PLATINUM THINKING

RAFAEL CALDERON JR

Copyright © 2016 Rafael Calderon Jr

All rights reserved.

ISBN: 1540424634
ISBN-13: 9781540424631

DEDICATION

To my daughter Jaiya a true blessing in my life and to the world may you manifest your full glory as a strong black woman and earth shaker and excel in your purpose. Your name means Victory and victorious you are.

To my daughter Kiara your beauty and ebony is radiant, your heart so sweet and full of joy, it is truly an inspiration to myself and to the world and I thank you. May God continue to bless you I love you and it is my hope that you will impact the world beyond your dreams.

CONTENTS

	Dedication	iii
	Contents	iv
	Preface	v
	Endorsements	vii
	Introduction	1
1	My Story	3
2	Provide Platinum Service	8
3	The Guest List	14
4	The Plan	20
	Pointers	26
	Conclusion	29
	About The Author	31
	Study Guide	33

Preface:

Professional business tactics is a crucial part of your career because this is a highly competitive profession. This book teaches you strategic methods and techniques that will equip you for this fast growing industry, prepare you for the challenges of life, encourage you to go higher than what your eyes can see and challenge you to believe more in yourself than you ever have.

Platinum thinking is designed to motivate you, condition and strengthen your mental bandwidth & manifesting powers and support you to live out your dream.

Endorsements

"Inspirational"! "Rafael starts with his own story then goes on to provide affirmations that can lead anybody to success not only in the barber industry but in any industry."

-Rosita Romero, Community Activist, Founder at
The Dominican Women's Development Center New York, NY

"Excellent Read!" "Brief but effective and powerful." "I think that this is a perfect resource for many of those who are in the beauty industry and other professions." "I think the structure of the book (meaty, concise, precise) will encourage and impact those who truly hear the message"

-Tiara Cottle, SLP, Founder at
SLP360 Miami, FL

"Rafael Calderon reveals the strategic influence wise and discerning men and women can have in the lives of those around them." "Allow his barber experience to alter your perspective and speak to your heart"

-Dr. Andre Sanders Sr. Pastor Kingdom Faith Global Ministries- KFGM Miami, FL

"This Book is packed with powerful principles to help you navigate your journey to success." "Highly recommended."

-Deryl S. Lampkin
Author of Deliver Us From Evil, Learning From The Past

Introduction:

The Gates Family has a 100 year plan for their family . What is your 100 year plan for your family?

"Do you have the mental band width to see into the future that far and create generational income for your seeds and loved ones?" –John Leslie Brown

Wow, that's deep never thought of that you might say to yourself.

If you feel the need to provide for those you love then you need to get lined up with your purpose.

They depend on it. But where do I start ? You may ask.

It's not going to be easy it's going to be hard but it's possible and if you have the will to do it you'll learn it's necessary.

If you believe that it's necessary then it's done.

The vision comes with pro vision all you have to do is take the leap and you'll grow wings on your way down. It takes courage and if others have done it why can't you.

Chapter 1

My story

By 2009 I've worked sales in Miami-Dade county for 15 years.

From children's books, to Kirby vacuums and from fire alarms to rendition perfumes I've done it all and well.

By mid-2009 I recorded my first gospel hip-hop cd 'RADICAL' Volume 1 and for a year and a half, sold over 10,000 copies at an average of $3.50 each.

This was my only source of income for those 18 months and all bills were paid $900 rent, car note, cell phone, car insurance, tithes, food, equipment for printing and burning cd's (I printed/labeled, burned and packaged all RADICAL Volume 1 cd's myself and kept a record), light bill etc.

The income was good and was picking up. With volume 2 ready to come out the studio I was moving up in the industry with ease. The weather in Miami-Dade however is rainy today, sunshine tomorrow and the rainy days in those days were drowning my business because my field was door to door.

I needed a stronger foundation so I chose to finally pursue my dream of becoming a barber.

Barbering was a longtime dream of mine, a passion and it's something that turns me on. What turns you on?

What turns you on because what I've done with this book is show you how you can begin to see the world on your terms from a perspective that will add zest to your life in this profession by the time you finish reading it.

Do not despise small beginnings (Zechariah 4:10) and so we are looking for people who want to learn, grow, excel and change the industry.

I want you to think about your goals if you don't have any start creating some now.

In 2010 after I graduated beauty school and got my master barber license it wasn't long before I excelled in this industry.

Today an educator, business owner, husband, grandfather, music writer, entrepreneur, author and motivator I want to tell you that your dreams are possible.

Chapter 2

Provide Platinum Service

One of the keys to effectively building a clientele base is excellent service.

One of my best friends theme for her business is not to give their clients what they want nor to please their clients but it's to amaze their clients.

If you want your business to grow then your service has to be amazing.

If you want tomorrow what others don't have you have to be willing to do today what others won't do.

Let's use the hot towel shave as an example and compare services. The national rate for a hot towel shave is $38 and the average tip is $5-$10 for this service.

The reason why most barber shops in your city has a lower price than the national average is because they are not equipped to perform this service correctly.

With its original intent the hot towel shave is designed to amaze and add value to the consumer and your business. The problem is that most professionals don't have the knowledge of performing it correctly.

A correct hot towel shave consists of the 14 shaving areas, proper strokes in each area and proper lathering and steaming.

This knowledge and its application is the difference between below average rates in shops and average to above average rates.

The more amazing your service the more gratuity the guest will show naturally and understand and appreciate the value of this service.

There's a Bahamian saying dress how you want to be addressed and so I dress all my clients as guests.

This way they'll be treated as such in my place of business aiding in the building and retention of my guest list.

Educate yourself or staff in proper servicing and you'll see your business grow.

Attitude is another major key to effectively building a guest list in this profession.

You have to believe that your goals are possible and must understand that the difference between a good day and a bad day is your attitude.

"Your altitude is determined by your attitude" –Zig Ziglar
With a positive attitude your dreams will begin to manifest.

Think about your goals again and visualize them accomplished now add to the accomplished goal. Now say to yourself it's possible.

The day you made up in your mind you wanted to become a professional was the day you entered into a race for territory. This race isn't for the swift but for those that can endure to the end and it is not going to be easy it is going to be hard.

Persistence breaks resistance and so you cannot stroll to your goal you have to fight for it, go day and night for it and it can be done and it will be done.

Never stop learning and advancing, go to seminars, expos, watch YouTube and Instagram videos, knowledge is the new currency.

Chapter 3

The Guest List

    Mastering the guest consultation is one of the secrets to retaining a successful guest list. During the guest consultation you have the opportunity to make an first and lasting impression.

    I've studied and learned that people will make judgements within the first five seconds of a interaction.

The first two seconds instinct is making up the mind, the next three seconds are reactions to the decision of the instinct. I encourage you to inherit a spirit of excellence for your life and business.

People don't plan to fail people fail to plan. Most people are trying to get through the day but true leaders are trying to get something out of the day.

What kind of impression are you making? Are you preparing yourself and staff daily to receive, service and amaze guests?

Are you just trying to make it through the day? To maintain a successful guest list your guests must always feel welcome and at home. Have the spirit of servitude.

My hope is that you manifest the industry changing leader seed inside of you and like mother said "become a pen in the hands of God and write a new chapter for your life"

–Mother Teresa

A friend of mine has a luxury barbershop in West Palm Beach, FL inside an office building.

The atmosphere in each area of the business is different.

The area where the guest consultation is adhered is: open but private, well lit, plenty of mirrors, product samples, hairstyle magazines and information for custom hair replacement systems in the form of brochures and books.

The shampoo bowl area has soft music, soft lights, soft colors and aromatherapy candles. The staff has a dress code that raises the bar and gives guests an experience to brag about.

"You don't get paid by the hour you get paid by how much value you can give in an hour"

-Jim Rohn

He mastered the guest consultation by making an impression with the environment first, a perfect aid as it sets the tone for the business.

In this office building where his shop is are dentist offices, doctor offices and law firm offices.

I'm proud of my friend and his great accomplishments so far. He raised the bar and set a new pace for his life and the industry.

Your average guest might choose average barbershops on average but the percentage of guest retention in average barbershops are below average.

You don't have to be great to get started but you have to get started to be great and when you start don't ever stop. In spite of your circumstances in order to achieve greatness, you have to get started.

Chapter 4

The Plan

"It is better to be prepared for an opportunity and not need one than to have an opportunity and not be prepared" –Whitney Young

Are you prepared mentally, physically, emotionally and spiritually to go above and beyond your comfort zone?

The reason why the great ones in history make such impact on the earth is because they are willing to die for what they believe in.

They are willing to go the extra mile and it is worth it to them.

Watch successful professionals in this industry and do what they do, study them because success leaves a trail.

"Sight is the function of the eyes but vision is the function of the heart" –Myles Munroe

I encourage you to live full but die empty. Remind yourself daily it's worth it.

I recently met a business owner that has 2 beauty salons on Miami's South Beach.

This young man studied cosmetology in Europe, he went to school for 4000 hours.

Even though he only needed 1800 hours to graduate, he decided to go back to school for another 2200 hours. To him it was worth it.

Are you doing what's worth it to you in spite of what other think, feel or say about you?

PLATINUM THINKING

He had a plan & 4 years after getting his cosmetology license he operates two locations in the heart of Miami's South Beach and he brings home a whopping $200,000 a year.

Have a plan and follow through with it, it's worth it.

"Education is the most powerful weapon that you can use to change the world"

-Nelson Mandela

There's greatness in you!

I encourage you make a 100 year plan, expand your vision, fulfill your purpose and manifest your glory to glory to glory.

"You can't be casual about your dreams or you'll become a casualty" -Les Brown

This goal this dream this idea this curriculum that you have for this industry and for the next generation of professionals, you have to own it and never let anyone take it from you.

Once manifested train the next generation on how to operate and manage your dream, your business, your idea.

Teach and train them how to troubleshoot your business in troubled times because if you don't they'll fail to keep it alive simply because they don't know how to.

This is imperative to your dream because without someone carrying it on your dream will die. Dreams are supposed to live on to the end of time.

Pointers

Use the law to your advantage for example patent, register and trademark your ideas, books, songs, inventions etc. Protect yourself and your future generational wealth with these assets readily available to you.

A great friend of mine who created a music beat and made money from it once told me "you don't know how good it feels to get a check in the mail from something you've created. I don't know how to explain it but I can describe it as a really really good feeling"

Yet another great friend of mine who created a song that was stolen and then made millions in 2015 told me "you don't know how bad it feels to have something you created taken away"

You see my first friend protected his ideas with copyrights but my second friend did not. He lost all rights reserved to his music even though he created it because he didn't protect it.

    Learn from others mistakes and avoid making the same mistake.

    Studies show that we have over 18 million to 25 million thoughts or ideas per year and 3-5 of those thoughts if we would act on it will become positive life changers in our lives and worth the investment.

    Write your ideas down in a journal, you can buy one at your local book store or choose from plenty of apps.

    Trust your heart and Lean not unto your own understanding (Proverbs 3:5) The provisions are already in place.

Conclusion

The beauty industry is a $95 billion a year industry and growing 7% every year.

Learning new skills, updating old systems, learning different tactics and techniques for problem solving, creating an innovative mindset, creating and trying new and improved products, tools, implements and equipment are priorities for staying in the now.

Your dreams are possible but you have to go after them.

Your goals are necessary but they depend on you.

Platinum Thinking In Your Life Starts Today, Take The Leap And With The Help Of God You'll Get It.

Follow us on Instagram
@PlatinumThinking
#PlatinumThinking

ABOUT THE AUTHOR

Rafael Calderon immersed himself within the Barber curriculum and became a graduate of Beauty Schools of America (BSA).

Following the accomplishment of his state board testing and licensure he has become Owner of Radical Cutz, LLC and a BSA Barber Instructor.

His mission is to educate others in the barber industry, build a successful business, and expand globally.

Mr. Calderon is a big dreamer, visionary, and talented leader. His teaching reflects a character that is vibrant, enthusiastic, capable, educated yet consistently learning, textbook and street smart.

Daily, Rafael continues his commission and passion in this industry, helping others excel towards their life long goals and dreams through service, teaching, mentoring, guiding and leading.

Platinum Thinking Study Guide

Preface:

1. What is a crucial part of your career?

_____

_____

2. Why?

_____

_____

_____

3. This book teaches you strategic methods and techniques that will

_____

_____

_____

_____

_____

4. Platinum thinking is designed to motivate you, condition and strengthen your mental bandwidth & manifesting powers and support you to live out your dream

(True or False)

Introduction:

1. The Gates Family has a _____ for their family .

2. What is your 100 year plan for your family?_____
_____

3. Who asked "Do you have the mental band width to see into the future that far and create generational income for your seeds and loved ones?"_____

_____

4. If you feel the need to provide for those you love then you need to get lined up with your_____

5. What's going to be hard?_____

_____

6. If you _____ that it's necessary then it's done.

7. Then it's what?_____

8. The _____ comes with_____
_____ all you have to do is take the leap and you'll grow wings on your way down.

9. What will it take?_____ and if others have done it why can't you.

Chapter 1
My story

1. I needed a _____ so I chose to finally pursue my
   _____

2. Barbering was a longtime dream of mine. What else?_____

3. What turns you on?_____

4. What turns you on because what I've done with this book is show you how you can begin to see _____ on your terms from a _____ that will add zest to your life in this profession by the time you finish reading it.

5. Do not despise small beginnings (Zechariah 4:10) and so we are looking for people who want to learn, _____excel and change the industry.

Platinum Thinking Activity 1

-Goal Development

Write down your goals and for each goal write 21 ideas or ways of accomplishing your goals

PLATINUM THINKING

Goal:_____

1. _____

2. _____

3. _____

4. _____

5. _____

6. _____

7. _____

8. _____

9. _____

10. _____

11. _____

12. _____

13. _____

14. _____

15. _____

16. _____

17. _____

18. _____

19. _____

20. _____

21. _____

PLATINUM THINKING

Goal: _____

1. _____

2. _____

3. _____

4. _____

5. _____

6. _____

7. _____

8. _____

9. _____

10. _____

11. _____

12. _____

13. _____

14. _____

15. _____

16. _____

17. _____

18. _____

19. _____

20. _____

21. _____

Your Dreams Are Possible.

Chapter 2

Provide Platinum Service

1. One of the keys to effectively building a clientele base is_____.

2. One of my best friends theme for her business is not to give their clients what they want nor to please their clients but it's to _____ their clients.

3. If you want your business to grow then your_____ _____.

4. If you want _____ what others don't have you have to be willing to do _____ what others won't do.

5. Why is it that most barber shops have lower prices than the national average?_____
   _____
   _____
   _____

6. With its original intent the hot towel shave is designed to_____ and add_____ to the consumer and your business.

PLATINUM THINKING

7. The problem is that most professionals don't have the_____
   _____
   _____.

8. This _____and its_____ is the difference between below average rates in shops and average to above average rates.

9. What's the Bahamian saying stated in this chapter?
   _____

10. Treating consumers as guests will do what?_____
    _____

11. What must you do to see your business grow?_____
_____

12. What is another major key to effectively building a guest list in this profession.?_____
_____

13. What is the difference between a good day and a bad day?_____

14. "Your_____ is determined by your attitude"
–Zig Ziglar

15. What must you have in order for your dreams to begin to manifest?_____
_____

16. This race isn't for the swift but _____
_____and it is not going to be easy it is going to be hard.

17. Never stop learning and advancing, go to seminars, expos, watch YouTube and Instagram videos, knowledge is_____
_____

Platinum Thinking Activity 2

-Goal Development Challenge

Most people are just trying to get through the day but true leaders are trying to get something out of the day. Write down seven goals that you want to accomplish tomorrow, read those goals tonight before going to bed and tomorrow morning after waking up and then check off each goal as they're accomplished throughout the day.

-Do this for 21 days

Tomorrows Goal List:

1. _____

2. _____

3. _____

4. _____

5. _____

6. _____

7. _____

Chapter 3
The Guest List

1. What is one of the secrets to retaining a successful guest list?_____ _____.

2. During the guest consultation you have the opportunity to make an _____ and
_____

I've studied and learned that people will make judgements within the first five seconds of a interaction.

3. What kind of impression are you making?

_____
_____
_____

PLATINUM THINKING

4. To maintain a successful guest list How must your guests always feel?

_____

5. What was the quote by Jim Rohn in this chapter?_____

_____

6. What aids the tone for business?_____

_____

7. You don't have to_____ to get started but you have to get started to be great and when you start don't ever stop.

8. What must you do in order to achieve greatness?_____
_____

Chapter 4
The Plan

1. Are you prepared mentally, physically, emotionally and spiritually to go above and beyond your comfort zone? Explain:_____
_____
_____
_____
_____
_____
_____

2. Why is it that the great ones in history make such impact on the earth? _____
_____

3. Why should we watch successful professionals in this industry and do what they do and study them?
_____
_____

4. I encourage you to _____ but _____.
Explain: _____
_____
_____
_____
_____
_____

5. What are you doing that's worth it to you in spite of what other think, feel or say about you?_____

_____
_____
_____
_____
_____

5. Have a _____ and _____ with it, it's worth it.

6. Who said, "Education is the most powerful weapon that you can use to change the world?"
_____

There's greatness in you!

"You can't be casual about your dreams or you'll become a casualty"
-Les Brown

7. What should you do with your goals, dreams and ideas?

_____
_____

8. Why will your staff fail to keep your business alive?

_____
_____

Dreams are supposed to live on to the end of time.

Pointers

1. How can you use the law to your advantage?_____
_____

-Goal Development Challenge

Call the following departments or visit their websites and explain the purpose for each office:

Copyright Office_____
_____
_____
_____

Patent Office _____

_____
_____
_____

Trademark Office _____

_____
_____
_____

2. In your own words why is it important to learn from others mistakes and avoid making the same mistakes? _____

_____
_____
_____
_____
_____

Define Provision:_____
_____
_____

Give 3 synonyms for provision
1. _____
2. _____
3. _____

Conclusion

1. How much is the beauty industry estimated worth?_____

2. How much is the beauty industry growing every year?_____

3. What are some of the priorities for staying in the now?_____
_____
_____
_____

4. Your dreams are possible but what must you do?_____

Your goals are necessary but they depend on you.

Platinum Thinking In Your Life Starts Today, Take The Leap And With The Help Of God You'll Get It.

www.ingramcontent.com/pod-product-compliance
Lightning Source LLC
Chambersburg PA
CBHW061206180526
45170CB00002B/989